Social welfare

P9-CFX-027

IMPROVING STUDY
AND HOMEWORK BEHAVIORS

By Steven Zifferblatt, Ph.D.
Stanford University
Stanford, California

RESEARCH PRESS COMPANY
2612 N. MATTIS AVE.
CHAMPAIGN, ILLINOIS 61820

CARNEGIE LIBRARY
LIVINGSTONE COLLEGE
SALISBURY, N. C. 28144

371.30281
Z 68

To my wife, Shelley

IMPROVING STUDY AND HOMEWORK BEHAVIORS

Copyright © 1970 by Research Press Company

All rights reserved. Printed in the United States of America. No part of this book may be re-produced by mimeograph or any other means without the written permission of the publisher. Excerpts may be printed in connection with published reviews in periodicals, without express permission.

Second Printing (Formerly called *You Can Help Your Child Improve Study and Homework Behaviors*).

ISBN 0-87822-012-7

Illustrated by RICK SPRINGER
Design by PAM THOMPSON

119 401

Excess stomach acidity?
Nagging backache?
Constant sniffles?
Early morning headaches?
A child not doing well in school?

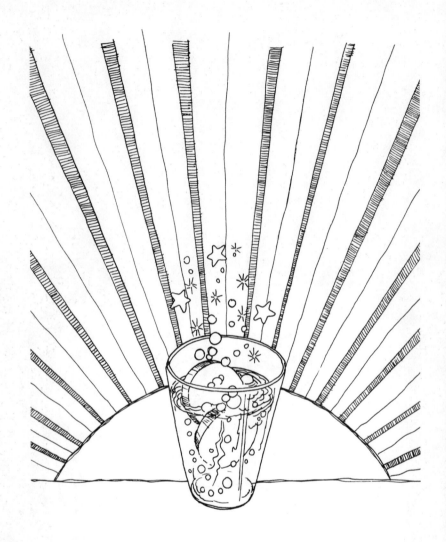

This Booklet
is Designed to Help
You Improve
Your Child's Study
and
Homework Behavior

the American Tragedy

Act One: Scene One

Setting: The living room at 7:30 P.M. Father reading newspaper and son watching television.

Father: "When are you going to do your homework?"

Son: "Don't worry about it, pop; I'll get it done right after this program."

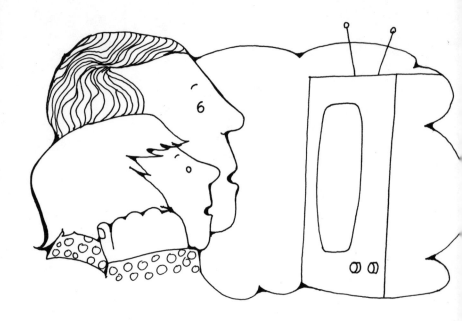

Act One: Scene Two

Setting: The living room at 8:30 P.M. Father watching television and son watching television.

Father: ''You said you were going to do your homework right after this program.''

Son: ''Look, will you get off my back? I'll get my work done before my classes in the morning!''

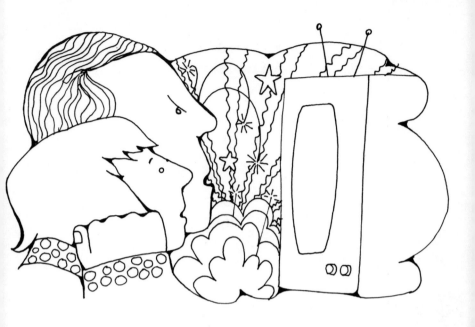

Act One: Scene Three

Setting: The living room in the evening a few weeks later.

Son: "Pop, I'm not doing too well in school. I just can't seem to get the hang of Spanish. It's driving me nuts. As a matter of fact I failed it for this marking period, but I did get by in my other subjects!"

Father: "You keep on handing me the same old story, but I know darn well that you have the brains to get better grades. You're just lazy and I'm going to fix your wagon once and for all. No television! No going out in the evenings for one month and I'm cutting your allowance! After dinner you are to go to your room and study until bedtime!"

Act Two: Scene One
Act Two: Scene Two
Act Two: Scene Three

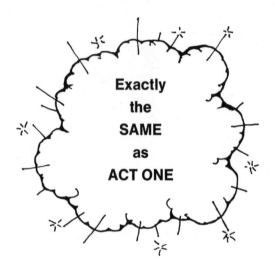

**Exactly
the
SAME
as
ACT ONE**

does the
AMERICAN TRAGEDY
sound
a little
familiar?

On the opposite page let's make a few
assumptions about the child's conversation
and have you make an evaluation . . .

ASSUMPTIONS

1. Your child is not at all worried about his grades, homework and study habits because he has an indifferent attitude toward school.

☐ true   ☐ false

2. The reason he jumps on your back and snaps at you when you mention school, or grades and studying is because you have hit upon a sore spot and he is sensitive about it.

☐ true   ☐ false

3. There's some kind of connection between your son's work at school, his social relationships and his interaction at home with his parents.

☐ true   ☐ false

4. Your consistent questioning and nagging always helps your child in doing his homework. That's why you do it.

☐ true   ☐ false

5. Time, logical thought, a calm attitude and past experience are behind your treatment of your child's difficulty in doing his homework.

☐ true   ☐ false

Correct choices: 1. (f), 2. (f), 3. (t), 4. (f), 5. (f)

PART ONE
Section A

What we have observed on the previous
pages occurs with a great number of our
Junior High School, High School and College
population. A child's difficulty in school
usually affects other areas of his life. Poor
work at school is not immediately forgotten
upon leaving school. It is on his mind
constantly and takes much of the enjoyment
away from everyday life. Imagine how your
child would behave at home with you if
he were an "A" student! Would there be
any difference? Would it affect his
friendships? Would it affect his vocational
plans? Would it affect his confidence?

If you try to make a "professional" effort
to help your child with his study and
homework behavior . . . can you do
something?

Yes, you can!

Knowledge of Geometry, or how to
conjugate a verb, or the chemical compounds
for photosynthesis . . .

are not necessary!

What is NECESSARY?

1. objectivity

2. consistency

3. selecting clear cut rules

4. selecting appropriate rules

5. emphasizing what your child is doing
   correctly, rather than incorrectly

These are necessary conditions and
characteristics which will help you succeed.

Let's take each one of those conditions
and characteristics, explain them and give
some situational examples. Then you can
try a few practical exercises.

A manager is OBJECTIVE . . .

To be
objective
you have to ask the
following questions
with regard to
YOUR BEHAVIOR
with your child:

1. Exactly what is happening at this moment?

2. How do I feel about the situation?

3. If this young person was someone I had never met before and I was asked to suggest a course of action after observing, what would I say?

4. *Putting everything else aside,* how can I help this young person achieve the desired goal?

To be
objective
you have to ask the following questions
about the BEHAVIOR OF YOUR CHILD:

1. What is his behavior at this moment?
2. What is the appropriate behavior for this situation?
3 Is there any difference between the two?
4. Is there any way I can capitalize on his behavior to guide him in performing the appropriate behavior?
5. How?
6. DO IT!

Remember ...   you are concerned with observable behavior:

1. Writing behavior (pencil movement on paper).
2. Reading behavior (eye contact with book in appropriate position).
3. Verbalizing correct answer behavior.

Just for practice, write down some observable behaviors at the dinner table:

1. _____

2. _____

3. _____

4. _____

Remember ...   you as well as others, must be able to see the behavior if it is to qualify as an observable behavior.

Let's return
to the point that
a manager is objective!

Situation: Your television-watching, homework-avoiding
son walks into the living room and asks you
for money to replace the television tube
in his room. You:

1. scream at him, call him a bum, get
   yourself upset and then give him the
   money.

2. give him the standard lecture on how
   he is messing up his life and someday
   he will be sorry and then give him
   the money.

3. punish him, refuse to fix the television,
   tell him it serves him right for spending
   so much time watching television and
   that he must return to his room
   immediately and study.

4. realize that eventually you are going to
   have to fix the television, but since he
   is asking a favor of you, you can ask
   something in return. He can help offset
   the cost of the tube with "payments"
   in the form of a number of appropriate
   homework behaviors until they equal
   the cost of the tube.

What is your choice?

Alternative #4 is most appropriate.

What are some of the important points that make alternative #4 different from the remaining choices?

1. _____

2. _____

3. _____

If you are still a little confused, go over the preceding pages.

A manager is CONSISTENT . . .

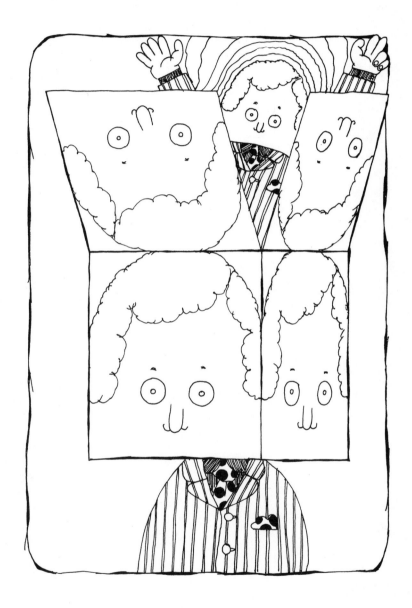

Consistency . . .

means *absolute* constant adherence to the agreement. To your son it means that he now knows exactly what to expect if his behavior is not of a certain specified nature; that he must face the consequences if he does not perform the exact behavior. It also means EVERY time and no exceptions!

(What do you think of people who don't keep their word, or change rules to suit their moods?)

Situation: Your son knows that he may come down
for a snack only after his homework is
completed and checked by you. This evening
he claims he is a little more hungry than
usual and would like to have his snack
before he completes his homework. A snack
has been a reward for homework behavior
and for the last week this has been the
pattern. You let him have his snack ahead
of time just this evening. A few days later
the same thing happens and he has his
snack at an earlier time before finishing
his homework. After a while he takes a snack
at any time.

What kind of behavior has been rewarded?

Appropriate?

Explain:

Inappropriate?

Explain:

By being inconsistent the rewarding of
appropriate behavior has been confused
with inappropriate behavior and reward loses
its effectiveness because *your son can't
count on you!* He does not know when he
will be rewarded for appropriate behavior
or get away with undesired behavior.

Situation: Your son runs into the house shouting that
he has earned an "A" on his big test this
week because of the study program you
have set up. You are very happy and proud.
Even though it is Thursday and both of you
have agreed, as part of the program, that
he is not to go out during the week in the
evening, he asks if he can visit a friend.

Alternatives: Build your own alternatives based upon
what we have discussed.

_____

_____

_____

_____

_____

_____

_____

A manager selects CLEAR-CUT rules . . .

Elements of
clear-cut rules:

If we are going to concentrate on changing
homework behavior we are probably going
to have to set up some rules that you and
your child will agree upon. He may dislike
them, but if they are clear-cut, it will be very
difficult for him to "wiggle" his way out of them.

You have a right to demand no more or
no less than what was *exactly* agreed upon.
If the rule is attainable and made easy
he will have little difficulty in performing
the desirable behavior. Reward will come
easy and he will look forward to performing
to receive the reward.

Choose the clear-cut rule:

(a) "I don't want you home too late this
weekend."
(b) "I want you home at 11:30 on Friday
evening and 12:30 on Saturday evening.

(a) "Try not to do a slipshod job on your
homework."
(b) "Finish the exact amount of written
work agreed upon in each of your subjects
this evening. Then I'd like to look at it
and quiz you on some of the points."

Each (b) response is clear-cut

22

A rule
specifies the
behavior that is
appropriate . . .

The behavior
can then be
reinforced.

Gradually reinforcement
controls behavior.

How are we doing?

Any questions?

1. _____

2. _____

3. _____

After you have written them down go back
to the preceding pages and see if you can
find ideas that will help you answer them.

Take a five-minute break now . . .

then continue!

A manager selects APPROPRIATE rules . . .

If the rule is extremely difficult to follow the chances are that your child will not make a good attempt to perform the behavior. It is thus very important to make sure that your child can actually do the work that the rule asks of him. If you ask for too much you might discourage him from doing anything at all. Start with a rule about study and homework which can be followed easily. After a while you can gradually increase the requirements.

Examples of appropriate rules:

After watching your child at his desk you observe that he reads about 6 pages an hour. (a) set up a rule that specifies at least 20 pages of reading.

(b) set up a rule that specifies at least 7 pages of reading.

Another observation you make is that he spends only one hour at his desk doing homework. (a) specify that he spend 3 hours at his desk every evening.

(b) specify that he spend one hour and 10 minutes every evening.

At the same time you observe that he does only 3 arithmetic problems correctly. (a) specify that 10 problems must be done correctly.

(b) specify that 4 problems must be done correctly.

each (b) response is appropriate.

Now,
try your hand at a few
practical situations:

Your son is trying to "stay in shape" and
wants to jog around the track. He can just
barely do one mile.

Rule for the week: _____

_____

You want to improve your vocabulary and
learn a few new words. Last night you tried
to learn 20 new words, but you only
remember 6 today.

Rule for the week:_____

_____

Remember . . . emphasize what your child is doing
correctly rather than pointing out what he
is doing incorrectly.

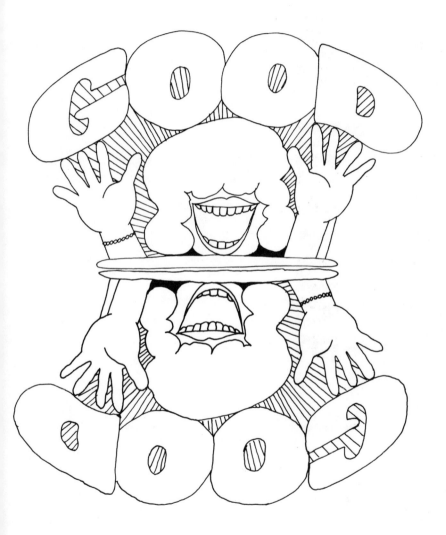

THINK POSITIVE

It is most important to emphasize the correct aspects of a persons's behavior, rather than the incorrect. Looking at what a person is doing correctly when making suggestions greatly increases the possibility that the person will take our "constructive suggestions" and follow them through. Most children are "on guard" constantly and very sensitive to their parents' suggestions. You can actually see your child "turn off" when you are about to criticize him. This is his way of not getting hurt when you are talking about something he is very sensitive to. Also being criticized by someone very close to him is difficult.

Thus, it is important, when you are trying to be objective and consistent to select clear-cut and appropriate rules and that you adopt a positive approach in trying to change study and homework behavior.

When observing a homework and study situation try to pick out a relevant behavior that is correct, even though infrequent, and emphasize what your child is doing correctly.

Remember ... there are always correct behaviors present and your job is to find them. (Finding and criticizing wrong behaviors is very easy and always a temptation.)

Now,
try your hand at a few
practical situations:

While observing your son at his desk you notice that in addition to looking at the book, he spends time doodling, looking about the room and just fidgeting. Your reaction to him is:

(a) point out that he spends too much time fidgeting.

(b) tell him he should not doodle so much.

(c) point out that he DOES look at his book for a short amount of time and this is good and to work on doing it for a longer period of time.

Correct choice (c)

Your son brings home his exam paper and on a 100 item test he has scored 64. He presents the paper to you very timidly. Your reaction is:

(a) point out that it was an easy test and everyone else did better than he did.

(b) look at the wrong answers and tell him he had better study and get them correct the next time.

(c) check over the correct answers and express approval. Ask what he did and studied to get them correct. Set up a procedure to capitalize on the things he did that resulted in correct work.

Correct choice (c)

You must try to achieve:

1. objectivity
2. consistency
3. selection of clear-cut rules
4. selection of appropriate rules
5. emphasis on what your child is doing correctly, rather than incorrectly.

PART ONE
Section B

You may have noticed that the word "behavior" and the word "observable" have been used on a number of occasions. These are most critical words . . .

BEHAVIOR!   OBSERVABLE!

Everything you do to help your child with his study and homework will deal with your actions to change his observable behavior.

What are some of his observable study and homework behaviors?

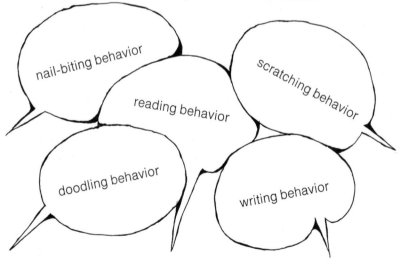

The important point to remember is that everything your child does can be observed by you. If he is alive (we must work under that assumption) he is behaving and it is observable.

Practical exercise: At the next meal make a deliberate effort to pick out as many observable behaviors as you can.

Example: Putting fork in mouth behavior, chewing behavior, passing food behavior, etc.

You should be able to pick out at least 25-100 observable behaviors.

(Think about it for a few minutes.)

Towards the end of this book you will be able to pick out your child's study and homework behaviors and help him work on changing or improving them. Make sure you know exactly what is meant by behavior!

What does "behavior" mean?

"Behavior" means:

1. _____ what your child is thinking about when he is supposed to be doing his homework.

2. _____ how your child feels when you ask him to go to his room.

3. _____ the actions or activities of your child at a particular time.

Correct choice (3)

At this point you can give yourself a pat on the back.

CONGRATULATIONS!!

You have just been promoted
You are now a . . .

MANAGER

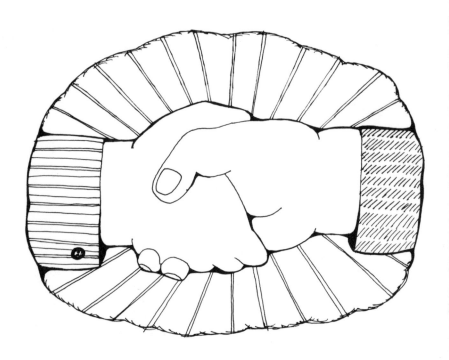

You have to know how to

MANAGE

your child's . . .

behavior

Manage . . .

manage . . .

manage . . .

manage . . .

What does "manage" mean?

33

"Manage" means:

1._____ to overshadow, to rule over, to occupy a commanding position.
2._____ to utter or use threats, to indicate possible danger, to offer punishment.
3._____ to help succeed in accomplishing a task, to guide, conduct or regulate, to handle or control in action or use.

Correct choice (3).

What does "behavior" mean?

"Behavior" means:

1._____ what your child is thinking about when he is supposed to be doing his homework.
2._____ how your child feels when you ask him to go to his room.
3._____ the actions or activities of your child at a particular time.

Correct choice (3).

If you didn't select #3 as the correct response to the previous questions check the selections again and learn the differences between the selections. Correct your "behavior." Contrast the alternatives and you should now understand what we mean when we speak of "behavior" and how to "manage" a situation.

What do we mean when we speak of behavior? (Discuss below)

_____

_____

_____

_____

_____

_____

What do we mean when we use the word manage? (Discuss below)

_____

_____

_____

_____

_____

_____

The type of behavior that is necessary to
manage your child's homework and studying
behavior will be . . .

your

ACTIONS

and

ACTIVITIES

in

MANAGING

behavior.

How are we going to do this?

TYPES AND AMOUNTS OF BEHAVIOR

we're going to concentrate on . . .

different

types

&

amounts

of

study

&

homework

behavior.

We might have the tendency to become emotionally involved with managing our child's homework and study behavior. This is quite natural. The important point to remember is that you are a . . .

. . . manager!

You can certainly remember times when you were very angry with your child. You were probably of little constructive help to him at that time. Anger is not one of the best states of mind for making effective decisions. Along a similar line of reasoning, happiness or enthusiasm also impair effective decision making because of the amount of emotion involved.

Remember . . .   your role is not that of emotionally involved parents, in this particular situation.

PART ONE
Section C

As a manager
you can now work under the 5
conditions mentioned in the first
part of the book.

What are they?

1._____

2._____

3._____

4._____

5._____

The most important feature of this experience for you is that you are now about to learn 3 scientifically-derived principles of behavior. Most likely you will have encountered them before in one form or another. The important point is that you will now be able to use them deliberately and place them in operation on your child's study and homework behavior.

The first principle of behavior is ...

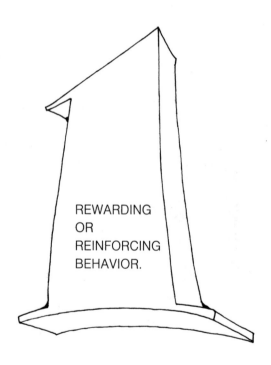

REWARDING
OR
REINFORCING
BEHAVIOR.

Behavior is rewarded or reinforced if:

1. the results of the behavior are satisfying or desirable.
2. there is verbal, or other signs of approval.
3. you get what you want from the behavior.
4. you avoid something unpleasant.

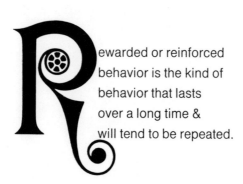

Rewarded or reinforced behavior is the kind of behavior that lasts over a long time & will tend to be repeated.

A manager objectively administers reward or reinforcement.

A person will tend to repeat a
behavior that makes him feel good:

If the consequences of the behavior
are desirable or positive.

If one gets something he wants.

If the behavior helps to avoid an
unpleasant task.

Thus a person repeats a behavior that is
rewarded or reinforced.

Situation: Your son rarely performs study or homework behaviors. Instead, he constantly makes excuses, watches television and delays doing his work.

Reward: Actually his homework and studying behaviors (inadequate as they are) are being rewarded or reinforced every evening.

How is this behavior being reinforced?

1. _____

2. _____

3. _____

Your son's inadequate homework
and studying behavior may be
reinforced in the following manner:

1. Hollering, nagging and screaming are
   ways that you are paying attention to him.
   They may be inappropriate behaviors on
   your part, but if he wants attention and
   nagging is "attention" then his behavior
   is being rewarded.
2. Recurrent behaviors or habits that are
   usually reinforced will always take place if
   they are always reinforced. Thus, he gets
   away with the same behavior over and over
   again.
3. Homework is a distasteful situation and
   avoiding it is rewarding. Thus, behavior
   used to avoid a situation is rewarding.

In many instances the difficulty lies
in the fact that inappropriate
behavior is rewarded behavior.

Thus, all behavior, whether
appropriate or inappropriate, if
rewarded, will tend to be repeated.

The trick is to reward appropriate behavior . . .

reading behavior
writing behavior
reviewing behavior
concentrating behavior
test-taking behavior

. . . not to reward inappropriate behavior
television-watching behavior
avoidance behavior
delaying behavior
poor work behavior

Most behavior is REWARDED or REINFORCED behavior.

If you walk down the same street to work, pick out a person whom you see every day on your way. When you walk by him and you both glance at each other finish your glance with a smile or a "hello." If you smile or greet him each day there will be a tendency for him to repeat the behavior because it is being reinforced. If you do not reinforce him the behavior will stop.

Example: When talking to a friend on the telephone try and reinforce an opinion he has. If you do this he will talk more and more concerning that opinion. If he ventures an opinion (behavior) and you do not try and reinforce it the behavior will stop.

Example: Quite often at a party or a gathering we reinforce other people's comments by nodding our head, saying "uh huh," you're right. What usually happens is that there is an increase in the behavior we have reinforced with the above. On the other hand, if we ignore what a person has said we will extinguish his behavior.

You can control behavior by:

giving reward
or
taking reward away

47

Example: Your son never comes to dinner on time. Every evening, you or your wife have to take extra time to call him again to the table. Actually, his behavior is being reinforced because it is exactly as expected and is a habit with all of you by now. He probably likes the extra attention that it gets him. Also, since you have done very little about it and permit the same behavior every evening, he does not think it is so bad.

Crucial questions: Is it your habit or his habit? Is the whole "play" one big habit? After you decide, what are you going to do to change the behavior?

Clue: Your son's behavior is being reinforced by your behavior. If you change the reward or response to the behavior, the behavior will change.

Alternatives: (a) By ignoring his coming to dinner late, you might change his behavior because you have changed the response or the reward.

(b) By objectively and quietly making the consequences of his behavior distasteful (no dinner if he comes late), his behavior will change rapidly.

(c) Perform alternative (b) and immediately reward him with a compliment when his behavior changes to coming to dinner on time. If he wanted attention, he will be getting it for appropriate behavior.

All three alternatives
on page 48
have good points.

What do they have in common?

What are some things that you can think of
to reward behavior?

1. _____

2. _____

3. _____

Examples: 1. compliment him,

2. stay up a little later

3. TV privileges

The second principle of behavior is:

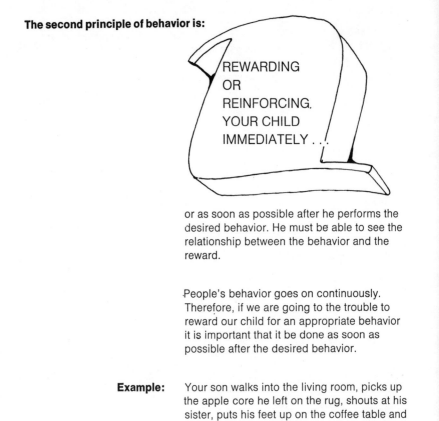

REWARDING
OR
REINFORCING.
YOUR CHILD
IMMEDIATELY . . .

or as soon as possible after he performs the desired behavior. He must be able to see the relationship between the behavior and the reward.

People's behavior goes on continuously. Therefore, if we are going to the trouble to reward our child for an appropriate behavior it is important that it be done as soon as possible after the desired behavior.

Example: Your son walks into the living room, picks up the apple core he left on the rug, shouts at his sister, puts his feet up on the coffee table and drops a candy wrapper on the chair. Then you reward him by commending him on his responsibility in picking up the core.

What might happen? _____

_____

_____

_____

_____

You might reinforce his putting his feet on the table and dropping the candy wrapper if you don't reinforce immediately after he picks up the apple core. In general, it is a good rule to reward as close to the desired behavior as possible.

If the reward is not immediate:

there may be a possibility that some of the consequent inappropriate behaviors may also have been reinforced. The closer you reward to the response the more powerful a meaning it conveys. Sometimes it is impossible to reward immediately after the behavior. This will suffice until the planned reward is present.

hen we reward behavior we must reward as immediately as possible!!

51

CARNEGIE LIBRARY
LIVINGSTONE COLLEGE
SALISBURY, N. C. 28144

The third principle of behavior is that of:

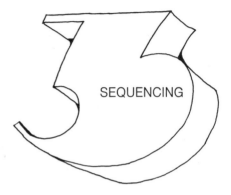

SEQUENCING

In many instances what we want our child to do is rather different from what he is doing now. For example, it is important that your child study two hours every evening. You observe that he only studies for ten minutes before he starts to fidget. This is a tricky situation. If you ask for too much "behavior" you will discourage him because the task is too big and overpowering. It also might be that he cannot perform the required behavior at this point.

If you use your managerial skills you can now get a "feel" for how much behavior your son can perform at this time. It is most important to make sure that your child can perform the behavior and receive a reward.

Start where he is, behaviorally, now. Reward him for what he is doing now and then three days by three days, or week by week increase the amount he has to behave to get a reward. This way he gains confidence in himself, since he can perform the behavior.

Examples of: sequencing

or gradually increasing the behavior.

You want to decrease your wife's
spending money:

    (a) take $15.00 away from her.

    (b) take $5.00 the first week and so on.

You want to build up your
physique:

    (a) attempt 50 push-ups, 50 sit-ups
immediately.

    (b) gradually build up your exercise
pattern attempting to increase it
every two days.

You want your son to change his
study behavior:

    (a) assign him 4 hours of study time right
away.

    (b) start him off with ten minutes per
subject and then slowly increase.

Each (b) response is
sequenced & appropriate.

Let's review page 25 for a moment

Principles
1. reward
2. immediacy
3. sequencing

See if you can remember the five conditions necessary to be a manager. . .

1._____

2._____

3._____

4._____

5._____

Did you miss any?
If you did, don't worry about it.
Reread pages 11-29.

The 3 principles of behavior are . . .

1._____

2._____

3._____

One word of caution! . . . There may be times when your child, as we do, gets tired of getting the same reward. You might remember to change the reward, if it is necessary (only if it is necessary). You can also increase or decrease the amount of reward.

Success is judged by whether you get the behavior you want AND using the least amount of reward to get it.

This is an important exercise, so take your
time and do it well. Try to pick out at least 25
behaviors and rewards that you can use
with your child.

Behaviors   **Rewards**

_____	1	_____
_____	2	_____
_____	3	_____
_____	4	_____
_____	5	_____
_____	6	_____
_____	7	_____
_____	8	_____
_____	9	_____
_____	10	_____
_____	11	_____
_____	12	_____
_____	13	_____
_____	14	_____
_____	15	_____
_____	16	_____
_____	17	_____
_____	18	_____
_____	19	_____
_____	20	_____
_____	21	_____
_____	22	_____
_____	23	_____
_____	24	_____
_____	25	_____

Let's double check at this point . . .

Combining both your skills as a manager and your knowledge of 3 principles of behavior is the basic requirement for helping your child with his study and homework behavior. Each one singly cannot do the job.

It is important that you are comfortable in your knowledge of the above, if you are to continue and learn a method for using these skills.

Ask yourself what each of the skills and principles mean:

Skills: objectivity

consistency

clear-cut rules

appropriate rules

emphasis on positive behavior

Principles: reward or reinforcement

immediacy

sequencing

If you remember your first principle of behavior you now know that it is important to make sure new behavior "pays off."

Reading this book is new behavior for you.

Take a well earned break!!

The next section of the book will give you a precise method for helping your child with study and homework behavior.

PART ONE
Section D

There are 6 steps to the plan of action:

1. observe
2. record
3. decide on goal
4. reward
5. record
6. evaluate

Let's take each one separately, explain it and cite a few examples. Then we'll put them all together and apply the entire method to a study problem.

The first step of our Plan of Action is:

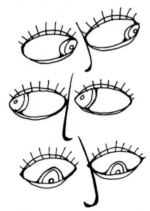

OBSERVE
Observe means to watch your child in the problem setting (usually the room where he does his work) and try to isolate the behavior with which you are going to help him.

Ask yourself this question while watching him: "What is he doing correctly, even if it's just in small amounts?" (think positive!)

If he is not doing anything correctly, ask yourself this question: "What is he doing incorrectly that I can change around and SHOW HIM how to do correctly?" It's important to remember that regardless of how right you are, if you don't make sure that your child can perform the required behavior, he may not succeed. This fits in with our previous discussion of *appropriate* and *clear-cut* rules.

Situation: Your child is trying to do some division
problems. During your observation time you
pinpoint the fact that he is not getting any
problems correct because he can't divide by
using decimal points. You realize that you
want to increase his correct answer bevavior
(you've observed that he really is trying and
not fooling around). The solution, of course,
is to increase his correct division behavior
with decimals. But, there is one catch. If you
just pointed out to him the desired behavior
it would not make any difference. You have to
make sure he can perform the behavior! Only
then will you be able to increase it.

Thus, your goals might be to: (a) increase his correct behavior after
showing him how to perform the
correct behavior.

(b) decrease his incorrect behavior.

Remember ...   make sure your child can do what you ask of
him!

Let's pinpoint one behavior and apply some
of the necessary principles we have learned.

Situation: Your child is having considerable difficulty
effectively doing his English homework. He
says he does the work, but his grades
certainly don't confirm this. You feel that the
behaviors involved are:

1. reading behavior

2. question-answering behavior

3. reviewing behavior.

Your Plan is to *manage* these three behaviors.

Your child will naturally think it strange that
your behavior toward him and his problem
has changed drastically. A brief discussion in
which you both recognize the problem and
agree to the need for change will render your
management more effective. And you've even
started to be objective.

The second step of our plan of action is:

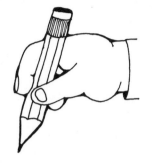

RECORD

An objective and precise individual must keep records of what is happening. Otherwise our procedures are subject to vagueness. We also might not remember what happened the previous day. Besides, there's nothing like "hard-nosed" data to prove our point. We expect doctors to make decisions about our health based upon precise data and we expect our children to be evaluated in school in the same manner. It's only fair that we do the same for our children.

In order to record something you have to be able to measure it. It's got to be "something-much, or so-much" of behavior.

Two very simple ways to measure and record behavior are:

1. how many times it occurs, e.g., 50 sentences
2. how long it occurs, e.g., 10 minutes of reading

All study and homework behaviors must be translated into either amount, or time.

Examples	Column A
6 correct examples	_____
5 minutes of arithmetic	_____
20 pages of history	_____
2 hours of reading	_____
10 minutes of doodling	_____
6 head scratches	_____

In column A write next to the above behaviors the type of measure used.

Exercise: Specify at least 6 behaviors performed by your child at the dinner table and the type of measure to be used.

Behavior   **Measure**

_____ 1. _____

_____ 2. _____

_____ 3. _____

_____ 4. _____

_____ 5. _____

_____ 6. _____

Sometimes either can be used, e.g., 50 sentences, or 2 minutes of reading. You have to choose which one is the most accurate and convenient to use.

What should you record on?

You might devise your own record sheet to suit the occasion. Or use the form on the following page . . .

BEHAVIOR CHART 2

CLASS:_____

	Date	Read	Question	Review
First				
Observation				
Average				
Goal				
Second				
Observation				

This is all you need to do the job. You will find a few extra Behavior Record forms at the back of this book.

While you are observing you might note the time and start recording. However you should record for a number of days just to get an accurate record of the amount, or time of the behavior you select. This is important because the behavior will vary. If you don't record for at least 3 days you might just have observed your child on a very "bad-day" and the amount of behavior observed and recorded is not an accurate reflection of his work. After 3 or 4 days you should be able to pinpoint the behavior you want to work with.

Remember ... if you pinpoint an inappropriate behavior you want to decrease it, but, at the same time you must give your child an appropriate behavior (tell him what and how to do it) and then increase it.

We always try to increase appropriate behavior!

Below is a sample Behavior Record Form.
Check it over . . .

	Date	Read	Question	Review
First				
Observation				

The third step of our plan is:

DECIDE ON GOAL

Deciding upon a suitable goal merely means that it is a realistic one, at least for the time being. You don't want to discourage your child. It's better to make the goal a little easier if you are not sure.

The importance of a goal is that it gives both you and your child something to "shoot for." It gives direction to your efforts and tells you when you have succeeded.

Situation: Let's set up a goal . . .

You have observed that your child finishes 6
algebra problems an evening. This is too
little. An algebra problem takes about 10
minutes to do and he spends 60 minutes on
algebra every evening. A realistic goal would
be:

(a) 6

(b) 8

(c) 12

Choice (b) would be most realistic. If he does
the problem correctly he will most likely take
less time, but not that much less. After a
while, as he gains practice and speed you can
again raise the amount of the goal to, perhaps
12. Also 12 might initially discourage him and
he might not even try to improve.

Remember . . .   it's time for you to set up goals as practice.

Make a decision about a goal based upon
your observations of what your child is
doing now.

At the next meal, make a few observations
about the amount of times the word "please"
is used by your child. Set up a little record for
a few days. Take a look at the record and set
up a realistic goal.

Try it!

The fourth step of our plan is:

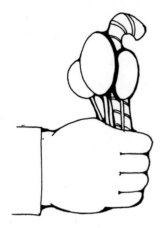

REWARD

A lot has been said about reward on pages 42-55.

Take a look at them again. Try and pick out what is happening right after the behavior you have observed and recorded. What is making it "pay off"?

Select an appropriate and clear-cut rule and use it!

There is absolutely nothing wrong with telling your child what he will get if he behaves. You've told him this before. Now the emphasis will be on positive behavior and you are objective and consistent with it. Don't forget this. It is very important. He is rewarded only if he performs the behavior.

For practice reread the examples described on pages 12-20.

The 5th step is: RECORD

What we mean by record is exactly the same
as in the second step.

Just keep a running acount of what is
happening on the same record form. If you
run out of space, use a new form.

By recording again, you can see if what you
have done has been effective.

Below is a behavior record form:

	Date	Read	Question	Review
Second				
Observation				

The final step in our plan is: EVALUATE

It means to check what you have done.
If it has been effective you might then make
plans for sequencing and further increase the
behavior.

On rare occasions, something goes
wrong with the way you use the
method. There are three big
checkpoints:

1. Does the reward work? Does your child
   like the reward? Sometimes what we think
   is a reward is not what our child enjoys.
   If you are in doubt, you might ask him.
2. Does your child know exactly what he is
   being rewarded for?
3. Can your child perform the behavior you
   are asking of him? It may be too much, too
   long, or too difficult.

Correct yourself!

Most errors in using this method are caught
at these checkpoints.

Briefly the 6 steps for increasing
your child's behavior are:

1. observe

2. record

3. decide on goal

4. _____

5. record

6. evaluate

(see if you can fill in the missing step)

69

Let's take a typical situation and apply the
six steps of the Plan of Action to increasing
a behavior.

Situation: Your child receives a poor grade in English.
His teacher points out that he has done poorly
on his big test covering three novels. The
teacher thinks he might be reading too slowly,
but is not sure.

1. Observation: You observe your son for four consecutive
days after discussing the problem. You
observe that he stays in his room for an hour
and he doodles a lot. He engages in very
little reading behavior. You then proceed to
make a record.

2. Record: The record for the amount of pages is on the
form below. You decided to record the
amount of pages read per hour because it was
precise. You could have recorded the amount
of time he read, but you could not always be
sure when he was actually reading.

CLASS: _English_

	Date	Read	Question	Review
First	10/30/70	6 pgs.		
Observation	10/31/70	8 pgs.		
	11/1/70	7 pgs.		

3. Goal: The record indicates that he averages about 7 pages in a one-hour session while reading "A Farewell To Arms." You don't want to discourage him. You also decide that you want to increase his page reading behavior. A realistic goal is ten pages of reading. You present it to him in the following manner:

a. The child will work only at his desk with no unimportant books or papers on it. There will be no distractions such as radio or television. He should read paragraph-by-paragraph, stopping at the end of it to ask himself if he knows the important points in it.

b. The *desired* behavior will be ten pages of reading per night. The reading is to be done in the above manner. The goal of ten pages should not be surpassed, nor should it be unattained. It should be exactly ten pages. For the first week only ten pages will be required for reward. In the second week, 20 pages are required. Third week —30 pages, etc.

c. Reading behavior will be performed at 7:00 P.M. and will continue until finished. This behavior should not be interrupted under any circumstances.

Average	11/1/70	7 pgs.		
Goal	11/1/70	10 pgs.		

4. Reward: If the specified goal is reached by using the desired behavior the child will be eligible to watch television for one-half hour that same evening only. (Other rewards might be percentage of allowance, car hours, bed-making or hobby privileges, evening hours, etc. (immediacy important)

5. Record: Continue taking an account on the Behavior Record Form. You obtain the following results:

	Date	Read	Question	Review
Second	11/2/70	8 pg.		
Observation	11/3/70	10 pgs		
	11/4/70	11 pgs		
	11/5/70	7 pgs		
	11/6/70	9 pgs		
	11/7/70	10 pgs		
	11/8/70	11 pgs		

6. Evaluate: You are positive of the results of your procedures, since you have a record to indicate that there has been a change. Start to think about sequencing.

Exercise: You have succeeded in increasing your child's study and homework behavior, but this has not helped his performance on tests. After observing again, you realize that he is reading, but not carefully. He cannot answer some questions that you ask him casually. You compliment him on the fact that he can answer some of them, but suggest that he might try to capitalize on what he is doing correctly and answer a few more. How might you improve his question-answering behavior?

Hint: Make a record of how many he answers correctly now, and increase the number.

Fill in a sample
Behavior Record Form
for questioning-answering behavior.
Then specify a goal and a reward.

	Date	Read	Question	Review
First				
Observation				

Goal

_____

_____

_____

_____

_____

Reward

_____

_____

_____

_____

_____

Record again and
Evaluate . . .

IT WORKS!

Now that you have had some practice with applying . . .

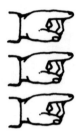 **managerial conditions**

principles of behavior

method for increasing behavior . . .

you are ready to try it with your child.

Take your time and think what has to be done!

Follow the steps given to you in the method!

Reread any points about which you are not sure.

 ou owe
our child
our best!

PART III
Section A

In order to give you an idea of what appropriate study behavior is, a complete method of study is to be presented. You may use any or all of it. There are others, and a teacher might also be of help in outlining a method that is suitable for your child. You may develop some ideas of your own after reading the method described on the following pages.

A Sample Method For Studying

**What are correct study and
homework behaviors?**

In order to write a plan of action and specify
clear-cut behaviors we must be aware of
these behaviors, how to put them together
and how to decide if they were performed
correctly.

Let's now sequence and specify the correct
behaviors when reading from a textbook or
other required sources of reading relevant to
assignments and studying.

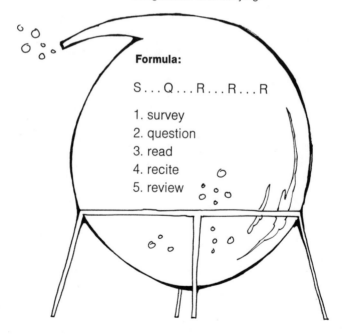

Formula:

S . . . Q . . . R . . . R . . . R

1. survey
2. question
3. read
4. recite
5. review

SURVEY Go through the chapter, page by page, getting an idea of what the chapter is about. Take careful note of the bold-faced type. Look at the italicized words. Look at the graphs, pictures and captions under them. Try to understand them. At the end of the chapter you should be able to answer a few general questions about the chapter:

(a) What is the chapter about?
(b) What is the chapter trying to emphasize?
(c) What area of the course does the chapter cover?

QUESTION Look at the bold-faced type (headings) introducing sections. Read the type carefully. Now change what it says into a question.

For example, change "The Campaigns of the War in the South" to . . .

"What were the campaigns in the South and what happened in each one?"

READ After you have formed the question, read the paragraph or section that is included under the bold-faced type. Read carefully the parts of the paragraphs that answer the question you made.

REVIEW After you are sure you know the answer to the question you formed from the bold-faced type, look away from the book and ask yourself the question again. Can you answer it? If you can, go on to the next section. If you cannot, go back and look at the answers and try again.

RECITE When you've finished the entire chapter in this manner take a little break. Then go over the chapter again by asking yourself the same questions that you formed before. Can you still answer them? If not, review again.

PART TWO
Section B

**Managing Behaviors
in More Than One School Subject**

We can control behavior in not only one subject but several. All we have to do is follow the plan of action for each subject.

When we are working with more than one subject
sequencing &
scheduling
are very important.

We might sequence by attempting to manage behavior in only one subject. Then as we obtain control of the behavior we might attack another subject. We then continue slowly and build up the behaviors and subject load.

Not only is the behavior change we are trying to manage difficult for us, it is difficult for our child. Think of the many times you knew the proper thing to do, but you just could not bring yourself to do it. It took a great effort on your part and it will also be the same for your child.

What does a weekly schedule look like?

It is a good idea to outline a weekly schedule with your child with both of you keeping a copy?

Try to write a schedule for managing behavior in one subject for the first week.

first week:

Monday

_____

_____

Tuesday

_____

_____

Write the schedule for the same subject for the second week.

second week:

Monday

_____

_____

Tuesday

_____

_____

sample weekly schedules

first week: Monday

10p. English - Quiz & reward
5 math Problems - Quiz & reward
1 chapter of Social Studies - Quiz & reward
1 Spanish lesson - Quiz & reward

Tues.-Fri.

Repeat
Possible weekend rewards

second week: Monday

15 p. English - Quiz & Reward
8 math problems - Quiz & Reward
2 Ch. Social Studies - Quiz & Reward
1 Spanish Lesson - Quiz & Reward

Tues.-Fri.

Repeat
Possible Weekend Rewards

don't be stingy with reward!

yet try not to "saturate"

In a particular situation you may decide to control and manage only one subject area and let the other areas roam free.

Remember ... GOING SLOWLY is a wiser procedure than overwhelming or discouraging your child. Inappropriate behavior will not respond to reinforcement!

You've set realistic and appropriate behaviors as goals. Because of this your child has reached them, been rewarded and will receive better grades in school. If you think your rewards have been effective, wait and see how really effective good grades are as a reward!

here is nothing that succeeds like success!

In using such a PLAN OF ACTION you have MANAGED you child's homework and study behavior.

PART TWO
Section C

We have dealt with consequences in relation to specifying the desired behavior and the conditions for being rewarded or not rewarded. It may be advisable to add to your plan of action a number of exact consequences if the appropriate behavior is not performed. This may be added incentive for the performance of desired behavior. As manager you have to make a decision as to its appropriateness. Sometimes, if consequences are too harsh, your child's first attempts might be destroyed. At any rate a manager with a positive emphasis on his "managing" has a greater effectiveness.

In many instances the manner in which you present your proposal to increase your child's study and homework behavior will be very important. You can well imagine that study and homework for a child not doing well is a distasteful situation and the presentation will have to be handled very gently. Think of a few topics, or areas of your life, that you are rather sensitive about. How would you react to someone approaching you to give you help?

One of the most important accomplishments you can achieve at first is to have your child agree that help is warranted. His consent and recognition are most important. They are the starting point of any action to be taken. After mutual recognition of the problem and observation you may then decide upon your plan of action. This also should be discussed with your child and consent obtained. Try not to give up quickly in obtaining his consent. You know him well. Use that knowledge to gain his consent.

Even after consent is obtained, following through on the plans by your son is difficult. He might have the best of intentions, but it is difficult to break a pattern of living, or in the language we have been using, a persistent behavior. Thus, your complete clarification of the procedure and agreement by both of you is important. In this way both of you know exactly what the other is responsible for doing. You have as much of a "behavioral obligation" as your son. In many instances having the agreement in written, rather than verbal, form is preferable. Your child might be more disposed to adhere to a written agreement, since it is set down in "black and white." Going a step further, you might have both your signatures on the written agreement, thus, resembling a legal contract between both of you. The persuasiveness of such a quasi-legal document is great and it makes many adolescents feel rather "grown-up." This type of document is known as a . . .

BEHAVIOR CONTRACT

You might draw up a behavior contract with your child after goals, behaviors and rewards are agreed upon.

A Behavior Contract: is a legal document that specifies the exact nature of the agreement between you and your son. Every aspect of the agreement should be included in detail! The contract should be signed, as in any other legal document, by all concerned parties and copies given to each party. As is typical of any other situation, consequences for failure to live up to the contract might be included.

What does a Behavior Contract look like?

Behavior Contract

I, _____ of _____ do
hereby enter into the following agreement with my parents. I will perform the behaviors stated below under all circumstances. In return I will receive such benefits as stipulated below. If any party is held in violation of the contract then the other party may no longer be held by the terms of this contract.

I agree to perform the following:

1. I will record, exactly, each homework assignment for each day of my classes every day in a small notebook. This notebook will be used by my parents and me in conjunction to plan the performing of my homework and related studying.

2. Each weekday evening a schedule of school work will be planned by my parents specifying exactly the amount of work to be accomplished and the manner in which it is to be done. A record of this plan is to be kept by both my parents and myself. Criteria for deciding my level of performance will be administered by my parents each evening in each subject scheduled for work that evening. The manner of the administration of the quiz will be decided upon conjunctively.

3. If the specified behaviors are performed correctly I will receive for each night of correct behavior:

   (a) the privilege of not making my bed the next morning.

   (b) a snack to be taken as scheduled in the following evening.

   (c) hours of watching television will be determined by the number of points earned each evening for quality of work. These points can be used only on the weekend following the homework week.

Failure to adhere to these conditions will result in the forfeiture of the above-stated privileges for the amount of time specified. Continued failure will result in the levying of an "allowance tax" which will be calculated by dividing the total allowance into fifths and for each evening I have not performed my behavior correctly I will be taxed one-fifth of my allowance. Extra work on weekends will result in a commensurate increase on the above scale.

This contract will commence on _____ and will be in effect for an indeterminate date.

(signed)_____, child

_____, parents

(date)_____.

Behavior Contract

I, _____ of _____ do hereby enter into the following agreement with my parents. I will perform the behaviors stated below under all circumstances. In return I will receive such benefits as stipulated below. If any party is held in violation of the contract then the other party may no longer be held by the terms of this contract.

I agree to perform the following:

1. I will record, exactly, each homework assignment for each day of my classes every day in a small notebook. This notebook will be used by my parents and me in conjunction to plan the performing of my homework and related studying.

2. Each weekday evening a schedule of school work will be planned by my parents specifying exactly the amount of work to be accomplished and the manner in which it is to be done. A record of this plan is to be kept by both my parents and myself. Criteria for deciding my level of performance will be administered by my parents each evening in each subject scheduled for work that evening. The manner of the administration of the quiz will be decided upon conjunctively.

3. If the specified behaviors are performed correctly I will receive for each night of correct behavior:

    (a) the privilege of not making my bed the next morning.

    (b) a snack to be taken as scheduled in the following evening.

    (c) hours of watching television will be determined by the number of points earned each evening for quality of work. These points can be used only on the weekend following the homework week.

Failure to adhere to these conditions will result in the forfeiture of the above-stated privileges for the amount of time specified. Continued failure will result in the levying of an "allowance tax" which will be calculated by dividing the total allowance into fifths and for each evening I have not performed my behavior correctly I will be taxed one-fifth of my allowance. Extra work on weekends will result in a commensurate increase on the above scale.

This contract will commence on _____ and will be in effect for an indeterminate date.

(signed) _____, child

_____, parents

Behavior Contract

I, _____ of _____ do hereby enter into the following agreement with my parents. I will perform the behaviors stated below under all circumstances. In return I will receive such benefits as stipulated below. If any party is held in violation of the contract then the other party may no longer be held by the terms of this contract.

I agree to perform the following:

1. I will record, exactly, each homework assignment for each day of my classes every day in a small notebook. This notebook will be used by my parents and me in conjunction to plan the performing of my homework and related studying.

2. Each weekday evening a schedule of school work will be planned by my parents specifying exactly the amount of work to be accomplished and the manner in which it is to be done. A record of this plan is to be kept by both my parents and myself. Criteria for deciding my level of performance will be administered by my parents each evening in each subject scheduled for work that evening. The manner of the administration of the quiz will be decided upon conjunctively.

3. If the specified behaviors are performed correctly I will receive for each night of correct behavior:

    (a) the privilege of not making my bed the next morning.

    (b) a snack to be taken as scheduled in the following evening.

    (c) hours of watching television will be determined by the number of points earned each evening for quality of work. These points can be used only on the weekend following the homework week.

Failure to adhere to these conditions will result in the forfeiture of the above-stated privileges for the amount of time specified. Continued failure will result in the levying of an "allowance tax" which will be calculated by dividing the total allowance into fifths and for each evening I have not performed my behavior correctly I will be taxed one-fifth of my allowance. Extra work on weekends will result in a commensurate increase on the above scale.

This contract will commence on _____ and will be in effect for an indeterminate date.

(signed)_____, child

_____, parents

BEHAVIOR CHART 2

CLASS: _____

	Date	Read	Question	Review
First				
Observation				
Average				
Goal				
Second				
Observation				

BEHAVIOR CHART 2

CLASS: _____

	Date	Read	Question	Review
First				
Observation				
Average				
Goal				
Second				
Observation				

BEHAVIOR CHART 2

CLASS: _____

	Date	Read	Question	Review
First				
Observation				
Average				
Goal				
Second				
Observation				

BEHAVIOR CHART 2

CLASS: _____

	Date	Read	Question	Review
First				
Observation				
Average				
Goal				
Second				
Observation				